Joseph Haydn

STABAT MATER

FOR FOUR PART CHORUS
FOUR SOLO VOICES
AND ORCHESTRA

EDITED BY
H. C. ROBBINS LANDON

Piano reduction by
Roderick Biss

FABER MUSIC LIMITED

First published in 1977 by Faber Music Ltd
Bloomsbury House 74–77 Great Russell Street London WC1B 3DA
Cover design by S & M Tucker
Printed in England by Caligraving Ltd

ISBN10: 0-571-50500-7
EAN13: 978-0-571-50500-5

To buy Faber Music publications or to find out about the full range of titles available
please contact your local music retailer or Faber Music sales enquiries:

Faber Music Limited, Burnt Mill, Elizabeth Way, Harlow, CM20 2HX England
Tel: +44 (0)1279 82 89 82 Fax: +44 (0)1279 82 89 83
sales@fabermusic.com fabermusic.com

Orchestra

2 OBOES doubling
2 COR ANGLAIS
BASSOON
ORGAN
STRINGS

Full Score and parts are available

Duration: *c.* 80 minutes

Foreword

In 1766, the Chief or *Ober-Capellmeister* of the Princely Esterházy musical establishment, Gregor Werner, died. Haydn, who had been engaged in 1761, had for the past five years been in charge of the instrumental music, while Werner had organized the church music. Upon Werner's death, Haydn was promoted to be full *Capellmeister* and took charge of the whole range of musical activity for the Esterházy court. 1766 proved to be a vital year altogether in Haydn's life, for it marked the inauguration of a new Castle called Eszterháza (or Esterház, or Estoras), round which the court life was to centre, except for a brief period in winter when the Prince went to Vienna to pay his respects to the Imperial Court, from 1766 to 1790.

The singers now came under Haydn's jurisdiction, which meant not only for church music but also for opera – then a new and exotic art-form for Eisenstadt (up to then the principal Esterházy court) and Eszterháza. In 1766, Haydn showed what he could do in two major vocal works: the large-scale cantata mass, lasting nearly two hours, entitled *Missa Cellensis in honorem Beatissimae Virginis Mariae*, the fragmentary autograph manuscript of which, including the signed and dated beginning, has just been discovered in Roumania;[1] and the *intermezzo*, *La canterina*, which was rehearsed (with costumes) in Eisenstadt and first given in the Archbishop's garden in Pressburg (now Bratislava).

The subsequent year, 1767, Haydn set to work on another major work for the Church: the *Stabat Mater*. We learn of its existence from a letter by Haydn to Anton Scheffstoss, "Secretaire" and Chief Bookkeeper of the Esterházy administration, which reads as follows:[2]

Eisenstadt, 20th March 1768.

Nobly born,
Highly respected Sir!

You will recall that last year I set to music with all my power the highly esteemed hymn, called Stabat Mater, and that I sent it to the great and world-celebrated Hasse[3] with no other intention than that in case, here and there, I had not expressed adequately words of such great importance, this lack could be rectified by a master so successful in all forms of music. But contrary to my merits, this unique artist honoured the work by inexpressible praise, and wished nothing more than to hear it performed with the good players it requires. Since, however, there is a great want of singers *utriusque generis* in Vienna, I would therefore humbly and obediently ask His Serene and Gracious Highness through you, Sir, to allow me, Weigl and his wife[4], and Friberth[5] to go to Vienna next Thursday, there on Friday afternoon at the FFr.: Miseric:[6] to further the honour of our gracious prince by the performance of his servant; we would return to Eisenstadt on Saturday evening.

---

[1]The Mass used to be formerly known as the *Missa Sanctae Caeciliae*, which turns out to be a spurious nineteenth-century title. The State Library in Bucharest kindly supplied photographs of the mass fragment, which is published in facsimile in *Haydn Yearbook IX* (Bryn Mawr and Vienna, 1973).

[2]*The Collected Correspondence and London Notebooks of Joseph Haydn*, edited and translated by H. C. Robbins Landon, London 1959, p. 8.

[3] J. A. Hasse (1699–1783), especially well known for his operas and church music. Hasse was in Vienna at that time, writing music for the Court Opera.

[4] Joseph Weigl, the 'cellist, who had joined the band in June, 1761. In 1764 he married Anna Maria Josepha, the daughter of Anton Scheffstoss; she had been engaged as soprano in the church choir in 1760. Haydn was devoted to the family and was godparent to their first child, Joseph (born 1766).

[5] Carl Friberth, tenor of the Esterházy *Capelle* from 1759 to 1776. Friberth also arranged and translated libretti; he wrote the word-book for Haydn's opera, *L'incontro improvviso*, in 1775.

[6] The Order of the Brothers of Mercy (German: *Barmherzige Brüder*), whose Viennese convent in the Leopoldstadt still exists; Haydn had played the organ there as a young man.

If His Highness so wishes, someone other than Friberth could easily be sent up. Dearest Mons. Scheffstoss, please expedite my request; I remain, with the most profound veneration,

Your nobly born Sir's
most devoted
JOSEPHUS HAYDN, [m.]pria.

P.S. My compliments to all the gentlemen. The promised Divertimenti[7] will surely be delivered to His Highness one of these next weeks.

We have an interesting account of the *Stabat Mater* from a letter by the Rev. Christian Ignatius Latrobe, the Moravian minister and composer, to Vincent Novello, dated 22 November 1828.[8] Latrobe describes his first meeting with Haydn, which took place sometime in 1791.

I was introduced to him [Haydn] by Dr. Burney, who well knew the value I should set upon the personal acquaintance of a man, whose Works I so greatly admired, and of which I may say, that they had been a feast to my soul. [There follows a description of their first meeting.] He gave me his direction & begged me to call on him whenever I pleased, which I considered the more condescending, as he could derive neither honour nor profit by my acquaintance. You may be sure I availed myself of the privilege, & believe, that we did not grow tired of each other's company. The same friendly intercourse between us was kept up during both first & second visits to England. . . .

He appeared to me to be a religious character, & not only attentive to the forms & usages of his own Church, but under the influence of a devotional spirit. This is felt by those, who understand the language of Music, in many parts of his Masses & other Compositions for the Church. I once observed to him, that having in the year 1779, when a youth, obtained the parts of his Stabat Mater from a friend, who had found means to procure them at Dresden, I made a score &, became enchanted with its beauty. The study of it, more than of any other Work, helped to form my taste, & make me more zealous in the pursuit of this noble science. He seemed delighted to hear my remarks on a Composition, which he declared to be one of his favourites, & added, that it was no wonder, that it partook of a religious fervor, for it had been composed in the performance of a religious Vow. He then gave me the following account of it. Sometime about the year 1770, (but as to the particular year, I am not sure) he was siezed [*sic*] with a violent disorder, which threatened his life. "I was", said he "not prepared to die, and prayed to God to have mercy on me & grant me recovery. I also vowed, that if I were restored to health, I would compose a Stabat Mater in honour of the blessed Virgin, as a token of thankfulness. My prayer was heard & I recovered. With a grateful sense of my duty, I cheerfully set about the performance of my Vow, & endeavoured to do it in my best manner. When finished, I sent the score to my dear old friend Hasse, then residing at Venice" (if I am right) [*recte*: Vienna]. "He returned me an answer which I shall preserve as a treasure to the end of my life. It [the *Stabat Mater*] is full of affection & truly religious feeling, for he was not only my musical, but my spiritual father. The Stabat Mater was performed at Vienna, both in the Imperial Chapel & at other Churches with acceptance, but I dedicated it to the Electress of Saxony [Maria Antonia Walpurgis, widow of Friedrich August II], who was an excellent judge in Music, & at Dresden it was done justice to."—The tears glistened in his eyes, while he gave me this account, of which I have remembered the very words.

In those days, it was not customary to print church music, and Haydn's *Stabat Mater* circulated for over a decade in manuscript; the dedication to the Electress of Saxony must have been on a (now lost) MS. copy. We know that Haydn conducted a performance at the Piaristenkirche in Vienna, and that the Benedictine Monastery of Göttweig on the Danube acquired the work; both these events took place in the 1770s. Next we hear of the *Stabat Mater* in Haydn's correspondence to his publishers, Artaria & Co., in Vienna. In a letter under date "Estoras" [Eszterháza], 27 May 1781, we read:

Now something from Paris. Monsieur Le Gros, Directeur of the Concert Spirituel, wrote me the most flattering things about my *Stabat Mater*, which was performed there four times with the greatest applause; the gentlemen asked permission to have it engraved. They made me an offer to

---

[7] Trios for the baryton, an instrument which Prince Nicolaus particularly liked.

[8] British Museum, Department of Manuscripts, Add. 11730 fol. 112. The Museum kindly supplied a photograph of the document.

engrave all my future works on the most favourable terms for myself, and were most surprised that I was so singularly successful in my vocal compositions; but I wasn't at all surprised, for they have not yet heard anything. If they only could hear my operetta *L'isola disabitata* and my most recent opera, *La fedeltà premiata,* I assure you that no such work has been heard in Paris up to now, nor perhaps in Vienna either; my misfortune is that I live in the country. [*Collected Correspondence*, p. 28.]

In the April 1781 issue of the *Mercure de France*, French readers will have noted a long article on Haydn's *Stabat Mater*, as performed at the Concert Spirituel, and a comparison of it with the famous work by Pergolesi, which Haydn, incidentally, will have known, *inter alia*, from a copy of the work in the Eisenstadt *Stadtpfarrkirche* (Parish Church, now Cathedral). As matters turned out, the *Stabat Mater* was printed in Paris that year by Sieber, and shortly afterwards it was performed in London at the Nobility's Concert and engraved there by John Bland in 1784. A German edition by Bossler followed a few years thereafter, and another by Schwickert in Leipzig.

The most widely circulated edition was the full score issued with Latin and German text by Breitkopf & Härtel at Easter, 1803. In fact Haydn offered a new revision of the work just as Breitkopf & Härtel had sent two complimentary copies of the new score to the composer. The new revision was by Haydn's pupil Sigismund Neukomm, and it consisted in adding a whole new set of wind instrument parts to the work; Haydn supervised the revision but took no active part in it. Breitkopf took the new revision but sold it only in MS. copies.[9]

More than twenty years ago, when preparing the first gramophone recording of the *Stabat Mater* for Vox Company, we became aware of the fact that there were grave textual deficiencies in the old Breitkopf score (which, meanwhile, had been re-edited and reprinted by the same firm). Even in bar two of the work, the ornament was missing (a particularly crucial one, which of course also appears later in the movement). For the recording, we consulted as many local Viennese copies as we could, but it was obvious to us that one day a new and critical edition would be required. In the course of the next two decades, we looked for an old and reliable text of the *Stabat Mater* and finally, in the Church of St. Michael's in Sopron (Oedenburg, the next large town to Eszterháza), we found a very old and textually most important copy of the work. It was in the organ loft, where we soon found first-hand evidence of a close connection between Eszterháza and St. Michael's Church: not only other works by Haydn, including the "Aria pro Adventu" *Ein' Magd, ein' Dienerin* owned by Franz Novothny (Novotny), the Princely Esterházy organist at Eisenstadt in the Castle Chapel;[10] but also a copy of another "Aria pro Adventu" by Carl Friberth, of whom Haydn speaks in the letter quoted above; this Aria is copied by none other than Haydn's personal copyist, Joseph Elssler, Senior (died 1782), and on paper from the Princely Esterházy paper mill at Lockenhaus.

The Oedenburg (Sopron) copy of the *Stabat Mater* is copied on Italian paper on 4^{0} format with the watermarks $^{cs}_{c}$ and three half-moons of decreasing size. It consists of the four solo vocal parts, the oboe parts (alternating with *cors anglais*), strings and "Organo o Cembalo". The *tutti* parts for the chorus are missing, which means in effect that the chorus of "Virgo Virginum" is no longer extant; but when we examined the church archives, it appeared to us possible that the missing parts might turn up. We had actually found the *Stabat Mater* in a pile of anonymous music. Textually, this MS. is of the utmost importance. It is obviously a fairly accurate copy of a now lost authentic set of parts (or even the autograph?): we find the typical Haydn ornament ✢ (see "Stabat", bar 2) which was usually misread by the copyists as *tr* (as sometimes happens in this MS., too). Similarly, the use of "l" in the organ (for unison) is a typical Haydnesque device which copyists liked to turn into tall staccati. The parts, on twelve-stave paper, are entitled: "Stabat Mater/Organo/ô/Cembalo", "Oboe Primo" ("Corno Inglese"), "Oboe Secundo" ("Corno Inglese"), "Stabat Mater/Violino Primo", "Stabat Mater/Violino 2do" "Stabat Mater/Viola obl:", "Stabat Mater/Violone"

---

[9] Hermann von Hase: *Joseph Haydn und Breitkopf &Härtel*, Leipzig 1909, pp. 49f.

[10] *Haydn Yearbook IV*, p. 16. Novothny died on 25 August 1773.

[= Contrabasso], "Soprano Conc^{to}", "Alto Conc^{to}", "Tenore Conc^{to}", Basso Conc^{to}". There is also a substitute "Oboe I" part for the "Corno Inglese" in the "Virgo Virginum"; probably there existed at one time oboe substitute parts for all the *cor anglais* sections. The substitute oboe part is by a different hand and was obviously added later. We shall refer to this source as **A**.

B is a set of parts by Johann Elssler, son of Joseph (whom we have mentioned), and now in the Esterházy Archives of the National Széchényi Library, Budapest, catalogued as Ms. mus. I. 160.[11] Its existence is closely bound up with the Neukomm version which, in turn, was planned as a celebration to welcome Prince Nicolaus II Esterházy back from Paris in the Autumn of 1803. On 20 August 1803,[12] Haydn's biographer G. A. Griesinger writes to Breitkopf & Härtel, "... He offers you a Stabat Mater which has been engraved in England but to which he has been for some weeks now adding several wind instruments, so that he can perform it when the Prince returns from London [*recte*: Paris] (he is expected daily)." In a further letter of 2 November we learn that the wind parts were added "by one of his pupils, Neukomm". The Prince returned on 27 August 1803 and Haydn was at Eisenstadt to conduct various pieces of music, including a Mass and Te Deum at the *Bergkirche* on Sunday, 28 August. Probably the *Stabat Mater* in its new form was performed during the following week.

Leaving apart the added wind instruments by Neukomm, which consist of one flute and pairs of clarinets, bassoons, horns, trumpets, three trombones and timpani, the text of the Eisenstadt *Stabat Mater* is relatively accurate. It is not known from which source Neukomm took his text: by this time ✛ has been Bowdlerized into *tr*, but otherwise Elssler's MS., though not as early chronologically or in the textual hierarchy as **A**, is a good and reliable copy which is, to some extent, an authentic text. Unfortunately, a German translation was added later, and the vocal parts often "adjusted"; even worse, the musical text was later arranged to agree with the Breitkopf score of 1803. Naturally, Elssler's original text was the one to which we refer in the notes. Of the parts, some are relatively un-edited, while others show much later revision; presumably the new arrangement was popular at Eisenstadt, and was also conducted by the later conductor, J. N. Hummel, who succeeded Haydn when the old composer was no longer able to sustain the exhausting position of musical director at Eisenstadt.

The Neukomm additions are skilfully made, but they raise the same problem as his wind band parts to the early Mass in F (*c.* 1749) or his revision of *Il ritorno di Tobia* (1774–5). Do we want to have Haydn's original score, or one "brought up to date" for performance in the early nineteenth century? Up to now, *Il ritorno di Tobia* was only available for practical performance in Neukomm's arrangement (Universal Edition), but it seems to us preferable on every count to print the original and authentic versions rather than these Neukomm arrangements. The addition of the wind, brass and kettledrum parts does not materially add to the *Stabat Mater*; on the contrary, they give a fake *Directoire* covering to what is basically an early Louis XVI piece. Of course Haydn took into consideration the small forces available to him at Eisenstadt when scoring the work, but the very economy suggests a singleminded purpose; after all, he could have used the available Eisenstadt bassoons and horns, if he had wanted to. In this connection, it is very likely that Haydn had bassoons doubling the bass line through much of the *Stabat Mater*; that was his practice at Eisenstadt in those days, as we know from the famous "Applausus" letter of 1768.

C is the printed score by Breitkopf, which has had very wide circulation. Many sets of parts were copied from it, *e.g.* the set of MS. parts in the Budapest Library catalogued as IV. 67. For the last century and a half, most performances of Haydn's *Stabat Mater* have been based on this Breitkopf score. In the circumstances, we have not thought it necessary to

---

[11] *Haydn Compositions in the Music Collection of the National Széchényi Library, Budapest*, Budapest 1960, p. 100.

[12] *Haydn Yearbook III*, 43f.

provide detailed textual commentary about the other printed editions (Sieber, Bland, Bossler, Schwickert) which are, like Breitkopf, unauthentic but, unlike Breitkopf, never achieved more than a circulation of relatively limited duration.

The title page of the Breitkopf score reads:

STABAT MATER
a 4 Voci
coll' accompagnamento dell' Orchestra
composto
da
G. Haydn.

Partitura.

Stabat Mater
von
J. Haydn
mit unterlegtem deutschen Texte.

Leipzig
bey Breitkopf und Härtel.

Pr. 2 Rthlr.

The score is printed in what was then known as "Typendruck" (a kind of musical typewriter), such as was used by the Leipzig firm for the "Oeuvres Complettes" of Haydn and Mozart and, perhaps best known, for the Haydn Masses which Breitkopf issued in the first part of the nineteenth century. The score of the *Stabat Mater* consists of ninety-four pages in tall folio and is remarkably free of printer's errors (as opposed to what might be called "source errors", *i.e.* mistakes which occurred without Breitkopf being able to know of them).

Haydn's *Stabat Mater* was the first vocal work from Eisenstadt (or Eszterháza) to make a lasting impact on musical Europe. We have only the Rev. Latrobe's evidence for Haydn's composing the work as a vow, but we know from several other sources that the composer was very ill. The sources are all rather vague, mentioning about 1770 as the date: all except for one, which is precise. Haydn's brother Michael wrote for, and obtained from Salzburg's Archbishop Siegismund von Schrattenbach (in whose employ Michael Haydn was), permission to visit his sick brother Joseph *in 1771*. Michael did not make the visit, presumably because Joseph had meanwhile recovered.[13]

Now it is hardly possible that (Joseph) Haydn can have composed the *Stabat Mater* as a vow for a sickness that occurred in 1771, since as we have seen he had composed the work four years earlier. Certainly Haydn composed the first of two Masses for Mariazell, a famous pilgrimage church in Styria, as some sort of vow, or perhaps as a private prayer of thanks, in the year 1766. Haydn tended to tell stories that always had elements of truth but with the chronology often mixed up; after all, in 1791 he was talking of works composed nearly a quarter of a century earlier.

---

[13] Hans Jancik: *Michael Haydn, Ein vergessener Meister*, Vienna 1952, p. 2:.2.

That the *Stabat Mater* shows a great and profound change *vis-à-vis* Haydn's earlier church music is clear; but the change is also reflected in all the church music of the period 1766–72 such as the *Salve Regina* of 1771 and the three Masses of the period: *Missa Cellensis* (1766), *Missa in honorem B.V.M.* known as the Great Organ Mass (*c.* 1768), *Missa Sancti Nicolai* (1772). It was, in brief, the period during which Haydn suddenly, even dramatically, rose from the mass of Austrian *Kleinmeister* to become one of Europe's leading composers. The thoughtful, delicate and at times joyful and dramatic *Stabat Mater* is the vocal work that established Haydn throughout Europe as a composer of religious music; the work's beauties have not dimmed in the more than two hundred years since it was first played at Eisenstadt.

We would like to thank most especially the National Library in Budapest which not only supplied all the MS. material to the *Stabat Mater* from their archives but also kindly arranged to have the Sopron (Oedenburg) copy photographed for us. We would also like to thank the British Broadcasting Corporation Library for photographing for us the Breitkopf score. The Bland print is owned by the editor, while the Sieber print was kindly supplied by the Bibliothèque Nationale in Paris.

A Critical Appendix appears in the Full Score

STABAT MATER

Edited by H.C. Robbins Landon

JOSEPH HAYDN
(1732-1809)

18
ro - sa, jux - ta cru - cem la - cri-mo - sa, la - cri-mo - sa,
22
la - - - cri - mo - sa, dum pen - de - bat fi - li - us,
26
dum pen - de - - - - - - - - - - - - - bat
29
TUTTI
Sta-bat ma - ter do - lo - ro - sa,
fi - - li-us.
Sta - bat ma - ter do - lo - ro - sa, ju - xta
sim.

32
ju - xta cru - cem la - cri - mo - - sa; dum pen - de - bat
ju - xta cru - cem la - cri - mo - - sa; dum pen - de - bat, dum pen -
ju - xta cru - cem la - cri - mo - - sa; dum pen - de - bat
cru - cem la - cri - mo - - sa; dum pen - de - - -
35
fi - li - us, dum pen - de - - - - - - -
de - - - bat fi - li - us, dum pen - de - bat,
fi - li - us, dum pen - de - bat, dum pen - de - - - -
- - - bat, dum pen - de - - - - - -
38
- - - bat fi - li - us, fi - - - li - us.
dum pen - de - bat, dum pen - de - bat fi - li - us.
- - - - - bat fi - - - li - us.
- - - - - bat fi - li - us, fi - li - us.

41
TENORE SOLO
fi - li - us, dum pen - de - bat, sta - - bat ma - ter do - lo -
p
45
- ro - sa, do - lo - ro - sa, ju - xta cru - cem la - cri - mo - sa, do - lo -
f
p
49
S.
A.
T.
B.
- ro - sa, dum pen - de - bat, dum pen - de - bat fi - li - us.
TUTTI p
Cu - jus a - ni - mam ge -
52
- men - tem, con - tri - sta - tem et do - len - tem, per - tran - si - vit
f

55
gla - di-us, per - tran si - vit gla - - - - di-us, cu - jus
gla - di-us, per - tran si - vit gla - - - - di-us,
gla - di-us, per - tran si - - vit gla - - - - di-us,
gla - di-us, per - tran si - - vit gla - - - di-us,
58
a - ni-mam con - tri-sta - tam per - tran-si - vit gla - -
ge-men - tem et do - len - tem, ge-men-tem, do-len-tem, per - tran-
ge-men - tem et do - len - tem, ge-men-tem, do-len-tem, per - tran-
ge-men - tem et do - len - tem, ge-men-tem, do-len-tem, per - tran-
62
- - - di - us, per - tran - si - vit, per-tran - si - - vit
-si - vit gla-di - us, per - tran - si - vit, per-tran - si - - vit
-si - vit gla-di - us, gla - - di - us, per - - tran -
-si - vit gla-di - us, gla - di - us, per - - tran -

(64)
gla - - di - us, per-tran-si-vit gla-di-us, gla - - di - us,
gla - - di - us, per - tran-si-vit gla-di-us, gla - - di - us,
-si - vit, per - tran-si-vit gla-di-us, gla - - di - us,
-si - vit, per - tran-si-vit gla-di-us, gla - - di - us,
67
per - tran-si - vit gla - di-us,
per - tran-si - vit gla - di - us,
per - tran - si - vit gla - di-us,
per - tran - si - vit gla - di - us,
70
pertran-si - vit gla - di - us.
per-tran-si - vit gla-di - us.
per-tran-si - vit gla - di - us.
per - tran - si - vit gla - di - us.
STAY UP
WATCH!
→p 13

II
Larghetto
ALTO SOLO
O quam tristis et af - fli - cta
f p
-SIT

45
fu - it il - la be - ne - di - cta, Ma - ter u - ni - ge - ni - ti.
53
O quam tri - stis et af - fli - cta fu - it il - la be - ne - di - cta,
61
quae moe - re - bat, et do - le - bat, et tre - me - - - bat,
68
dum vi - de - bat na - ti pœ - nas, na - ti pœ - nas in - cly -
75
- ti, na - ti pœ - nas, na - ti pœ - - - - - nas
fp
f
p

84
in - cly - ti.
92
99
104
O, o quam
111
tri - stis et af - fli - cta, o quam tri - stis et af - fli - cta

118
fu - it il - la be - ne - di - cta, Ma - ter u - ni -
[𝄵]
p
125
- ge - ni - ti, u - ni - ge - ni - ti! Quæ moe - re - bat, et do - le - bat,
p
132
et tre - me - bat, dum vi - de - bat na - ti pœ - nas, pœ - nas
139
in - cly - ti. Quae moe - re - bat, et do - le - bat,
[𝄵]
f
p
145
et tre - me - bat, dum vi - de - bat na - ti poe - nas,

152

na - ti poe - nas in - cly - ti, na - ti poe - nas, na - ti

159

poe - - - - - - nas, na - ti poe - -

fz *p*

167

- - - - - nas,

f *p* *f*

174

poe - nas in - cly - ti.

tr

f *p* *f* *p* *f* *p* *f* *p* *f* *p* *f* *p* *f*

184

STAND

p *f*

191

III
Lento
TUTTI
SOPRANO
ALTO
TENORE
BASSO
Quis, quis, quis est ho-mo, quis est
Quis, quis, quis est ho-mo, quis est
Quis, quis, quis est ho-mo, quis est
Quis, quis, quis est ho-mo. quis est
Lento
ho - mo, qui non fle - ret, qui non
ho - mo, qui non fle - ret,
ho - mo, qui non fle - ret, qui non
ho - mo, qui non fle - ret, quis est ho-mo,
(6)
fle - - - ret, qui non fle - ret, Chri - sti Ma - trem si vi - de - ret, qui non
qui non fle - ret, non fle - ret, Chri - sti Ma - trem si vi - de - ret, qui non
fle - - - ret, qui non fle - ret, Chri - sti Ma - trem si vi - de - ret, qui non
qui non fle - ret, non fle - ret, Chri - sti Ma - trem si vi - de - ret, qui non
[sim.]

9
fle - ret, si vi - de - ret,
fle - ret, si vi - de - ret,
fle - ret, si vi - de - ret,
fle - ret, si vi - de - ret, in tan - to, in tan - to sup -
11
in tan - to, in
-pli - - ci - o?
(12)
in
tan - to sup - pli - - - ci - o?
Quis, quis, quis est ho - mo,

14
tan - to, in tan - to sup - pli - - ci -
Quis, quis est ho - - - - -
qui non fle - ret, Chri - sti Ma - trem si vi -
(15)
f
in tan - to, in tan - to sup -
-o? Quis, qui non
mo, qui non fle - ret, Chri - sti
-de - ret in tan - to, in tan - to sup -
17
-pli - - ci - o?
fle - - - ret, in
Ma - trem si vi - de - ret, in tan - to, in
-pli - ci - o, in tan - to, in

18
Quis, qui non fle - - - ret, in
tan - to sup - pli - - ci - o,
tan - to sup - pli - ci - o,
tan - to sup - pli - - - ci - o,
20
tan - to, in tan - to sup - pli - ci - o, in
in tan - to, in tan - - - - - -
in tan - - - - - -
in tan - to, in tan - - - - - -
22
tan - - to sup - pli - ci - o?
- - to, in tan - to sup - pli - ci - o?
- - to, in tan - to sup - pli - - ci - o?
- - - - - - to sup - pli - - ci - o?

IV
Moderato
SOPRANO SOLO
Quis non pos - set con - tri - sta - ri, pi - am Ma - trem
4
con - tem-pla-ri, do-len - tem, do - len - tem cum fi - li - o? Quis non pos - set
8
con - tri-sta-ri, pi - am Ma - trem con - tem - pla -
11
14
- ri, con-tem - pla - ri, do - len - tem cum Fi - li-o, cum Fi - li - o? Quis,

18
quis non pos-set
con - tri - sta-ri, con - tem - pla-ri,
do - len - tem cum
p
21
Fi - li-o, cum Fi - li - o,
do - len - - - - tem cum
24
Fi - li - o?
f
27
30
f
p

34
Quis non pos - set con - tri - sta - ri,
f
tr
p
38
pi - am Ma - trem con - tem-pla - ri, quis non pos - set
3
41
con - tri-sta-ri, pi - am Ma - trem
3
6
p
44
con - tem - pla
6
47
ri do -
cresc.
f
p

51
-len - tem cum Fi-li-o, cum Fi - li-o? Quis non pos-set con-tri-sta-ri, pi-am
54
Ma-trem con-tem-pla - ri do - len - - tem cum Fi-li-o?
f
57
Quis non pos-set con - tem - pla-ri do-len - tem cum Fi-li-o, cum fi - li -
p
60
-o, do-len - - - tem cum Fi - li - o,
fz
f
64
do - len - tem cum Fi - li - o?
f

67
71
V
Allegro ma non troppo
BASSO SOLO
Pro pec-ca-tis su-æ gen-tis,
6
pro pec-ca-tis su-æ gen-tis, su-ae gen-tis
9
vi-dit Je-sum in tor-
13
-men-tis, in tor-

16
-men - tis, in tor - men - tis, tor -
19
-men - tis et fla - gel - lis, fla-gel - lis sub - di - tum,
f
p
f
p
f
24
et fla-gel - - - lis, et fla-gel - - - - - - -
p
28
- lis, fla - gel - lis sub - - di - tum.
mf
f
32
Pro pec-ca - tis su - ae gen - tis,
3
p
f
3

36
pro pec-ca-tis su-ae gen-tis,
p
f
40
pro pec-ca-tis su-ae gen-tis, pro pec-ca-tis su-ae gen-tis
p
3
f
44
vi-dit Je-sum in tor-
p
48
-men-tis, in tor-
51
-men-tis, in tor-men-tis, tor-men-tis

55
et fla - gel - lis, fla-gel - - lis sub - di - tum,
59
et fla-gel - - lis, et fla-gel - - - -
63
- lis, fla-gel - lis sub - - di - tum,
66
et fla - gel - lis, fla-gel - lis, fla gel - lis sub - di -
70
tum.

VI Lento e maestoso

19
dum e - mi - sit spi - ri - tum, dum e - mi - sit, dum e - mi - sit
fz
fz
23
tr
spi - ri - tum.
f
p
f
3
26
p
f
30
p
Vi - dit su - um dul - cem na - tum, dul - cem na - tum
33
mo - ri - en - tem de - so - la - tum, mo - ri - en - tem dc - so - la - tum,

37
dum e-mi - sit spi-ri-tum, Vi - dit su - um dul - cem na - tum,
sim.
41
dul - cem na - - tum, dul-cem na - tum, dum e - mi - sit, e - mi - sit
pp
45
spi - ri - tum, dum e - mi - sit, dum e - mi - sit, dum e-mi - sit
poco f fz fz fz fz f p
49
spi - ri-tum, dum e - mi - sit spi - ri - tum.
f f p
53
f p
56
STAND
f p f p

VII
Allegretto
SOPRANO
ALTO
TENORE
BASSO
(poco f)
E - ia Ma - ter, fons a - mo - ris,
Allegretto
(poco f)
tr
8
e - ia Ma - ter, fons a - mo - ris me sen - ti - re vim do -
e - ia Ma - ter, fons a - mo - ris me sen - ti - re
e - ia Ma - ter, fons a - mo - ris me sen - ti - re
e - ia Ma - ter, fons a - mo - ris me sen - ti - re
16
- lo - ris fac ut te - cum, te - cum lu - ge - am. E - ia
vim do - lo - ris fac ut te - cum lu - ge - am.
vim do - lo - ris fac ut te - cum lu - ge - am. E - ia Ma - ter,
vim do - lo - ris fac ut te - cum lu - ge - am. E - ia Ma - ter, fons a -
f p f p (poco f)

25

Ma - ter, fons a - mo - ris, e - ia Ma - - ter, fons a - mo - ris

e - ia Ma - ter, fons a - mo - ris, e - ia Ma - ter, fons a - mo - ris

fons a - mo - ris, fons a - mo - ris, e - ia Ma - ter, fons a - mo - ris

mo - ris, fons a - mo - ris, e - ia Ma - ter, fons a - mo - ris

33

me sen - ti - re vim do - lo - ris, vim

me sen - ti - re vim do - lo - ris, vim

me sen - ti - re vim do - lo - ris, vim

me sen - ti - re vim do - lo - ris, vim

f p f p f p f p f p

40

do - lo - ris, vim do - lo - ris fac ut te - cum,

do - lo - ris, vim do - lo - ris fac ut te - cum,

do - lo - ris, vim do - lo - ris fac ut te - cum,

do - lo - ris, vim do - lo - ris fac ut te - cum,

f p f p f p f fz

48
fac ut te - cum lu - ge - am, fac ut te - cum, fac ut te - cum
fac ut te - cum lu - ge - am, fac ut te - cum, fac ut te - cum
fac ut te - cum lu - ge - am, fac ut te - cum, fac ut te - cum
fac ut te - cum lu - ge - am, fac ut te - cum, fac ut te - cum
57
lu - - ge - - am, fac ut te - cum, fac ut
lu - - ge - - am, fac ut te - cum, fac ut
lu - - ge - - am, fac ut te - cum, fac ut
lu - - ge - - am, fac ut te - cum, fac ut
66
te - cum lu - ge - am.
te - cum lu - ge - am.
te - cum lu - ge - am.
te - cum lu - ge - am.

74

Fac ut ar - de - at — cor me - um in a - man - do Chri - stum De - um, in a -

Fac ut ar - de - at — cor me - um in a - man - do Chri - stum De - um, in a -

Fac ut ar - de - at — cor me - um in a - man - do Chri - stum De - um, in a -

Fac ut ar - de - at — cor me - um in a - man - do Chri - stum De - um, in a -

mf

83

- man - do Chri - stum De - um, ut si - bi, ut si - bi com -

- man - do Chri - stum De - um, ut si - bi, ut

- man - do Chri - stum De - um, ut si - bi, ut si - bi com - pla - ce -

- man - do Chri - stum De - um, ut si - bi, ut si - bi com - pla - ce -

tr

92

- pla - - - - - - - - - ce - am,

si - bi com - pla - - - - - - ce - am, ut *mf*

- am, com - pla - - - - - - ce - am,

- am, com - pla - - - - - - ce - am, ut *mf*

mf

100
mf
ut si - bi com - pla - - - - ce - am, fac, fac,
si - bi com - pla - - - - - ce - am, fac, fac,
mf
ut si - bi com - pla - - ce - am, fac, fac,
si - bi com - pla - - - - - ce - am, fac, fac,
109
p
fac, ut si - bi, fac, ut si - bi com - pla - ce - am, fac, ut te - cum fac, ut
fac, ut si - bi, fac, ut si - bi com - pla - ce - am, fac, ut te - cum fac, ut
fac, ut si - bi, fac, ut si - bi com - pla - ce - am, fac, ut te - cum fac, ut
fac, ut si - bi, fac, ut si - bi com - pla - ce - am, fac, ut te - cum fac, ut
f p f p poco f p
119
f
te - cum lu - - - - ge - am, fac, ut si - bi, fac, ut
te - cum lu - - - - ge - am, fac, ut si - bi, fac, ut
te - cum lu - - - - ge - am, fac, ut si - bi, fac, ut
te - cum lu - - - - ge - am, fac, ut si - bi, fac, ut

SIT→p.43

129
si - bi com - pla - ce - am.
si - bi com - pla - ce - am.
si - bi com - pla - ce - am.
si - bi com - pla - ce - am.
VIII DUETTO
Larghetto
p dolce
f
p
8
f
f
14
p
18
SOPRANO SOLO
San cta
f
f
p

24
Ma-ter, i - stud a-gas, cru - ci - fi - xi fi - ge pla-gas
31
cor - di me - o va-li-de, cor-di me-o, cor - di me-o va-li-
38
-de, cor - di me - o va -
poco f
p
(sim.)
43
48
- li-de, cor - di me - o va - li - de, cor-di
f
p
(p)

55
me-o va - - - li-de.
TENORE SOLO
San - cta ma-ter i-stud a-gas
63
cru-ci-fi - xi fi - ge pla-gas cor - di me - o va-li-de,
71
cor-di me-o, cor-di me-o va-li-de, cor-di
poco f
p
(sim.)
78
me - o va - - - - - - - - -
84
- - - - - li-de, cor - di me - o va-li-de, cor-di

92
Tu - i na - ți _ vul - ne - ra - ti,
me - o _ va - - - - - li - de. Tam di -
sim.
98
poe - nas me - cum, poe - nas me - cum, poe - nas
gna - ti _ pro me pa - ti, poe - nas me - cum, poe - nas me - cum,
104
me - cum di - vi - de, poe - nas me - cum, poe - nas
me - cum di - vi - de, poe - nas me - cum,
f
p
110
me - - cum di - vi - de, poe - nas me - cum, poe - nas me - cum _ di - vi - de,
me - - cum di - vi - de, poe - nas me - cum, poe - nas me - cum _ di - vi - de,

117
poe - nas me - cum di - - vi - de.
poe - nas me - cum di - vi - de.
122
San - cta
128
Ma - ter, i - stud a - gas, cru - ci -
San - cta Ma - ter, i - stud a - gas, cru - ci -
134
- fi - xi fi - ge pla - gas cor - di me - o va - - - - -
- fi - xi fi - ge pla - gas cor - di me - o va - - - -

140
li - de, cor - di me - o
li - de, cor - di me - o
tr
147
va - li - de. Tu - i na - ti vul - ne - ra - ti,
va - li - de. Tam di -
poco f
p sim.
153
poe-nas me-cum, poe-nas me - cum di - vi-de,
-gna - ti pro me pa - ti, poe-nas me - cum di - vi-de,
f
159
poe - nas me-cum, poe - nas me - - - - - cum,
poe - nas me-cum, me - - - - cum,
p
f

166
poe - nas me - cum di - vi - de.
poe - nas me - cum di - vi - de.
172
176
IX
Lachrymoso
p sempre legato
3
6

8
ALTO SOLO
Fac me
11
ve-re te-cum fle-re, te-cum fle-re
cru - ci-fi - xo
14
con - do-le-re, do-nec e-go, do-nec e - go vi - xe - ro. Fac me
17
ve-re te-cum fle-re cru-ci-fi-xo con-do-le-re, con-do - le-re, do-nec e-go, do-nec
20
e-go, do-nec e - go vi - xe - ro, do-nec e-go, do-nec e

23
- - - go vi - xe - ro.
tr
f
25
Ju - xta cru - cem
p
28
te-cum, te-cum sta-re, et me ti-bi so-ci-a-re in plan-ctu de-
3
31
-si-de-ro, in plan - ctu de-si-de-ro. Ju - xta cru-cem te-cum sta-re, et me
34
ti - bi so-ci-a-re in plan - ctu de - si-de-ro, in

36
plan - - - - - - - ctu de - si - de-ro, et me
39
ti-bi so-ci-a-re in plan - ctu de-si - de - ro, in plan-ctu, in
42
plan - - - - - ctu, in plan - - ctu, in
44
plan-ctu de-si - de-ro.
47
49

STAND solo quartet

X QUARTETTO con CORO

44
SOPRANO SOLO
Vir - go vir - gi - num prae - cla - ra, mi - hi jam non sis a -
sis a - ma - ra, mi - hi non sis a - ma - ra, non, mi - hi non sis a -
non sis a - ma - ra, mi - hi non sis a -
- num prae - cla - ra, mi - hi jam non sis a - ma - ra, a - ma -
53
- ma - ra, fac me te - cum plan - ge - re.
- ma - ra, fac me te - cum plan - ge - re.
- ma - ra, fac me te - cum plan - ge - re.
- ra, fac me te - cum plan - ge - re.
CORO
Fac, fac, fac,

62
Vir - go, vir - go vir - gi - num præ - cla - ra, mi - hi, mi - hi jam non sis a - ma - ra,
Vir - go, vir - go vir - gi - num præ - cla - ra, mi - hi, mi - hi jam non sis a - ma - ra,
Vir - go vir - gi - num præ - cla - ra, mi - hi jam nón sis a - ma - ra,
Vir - go, vir-go præ - cla - ra, mi - hi non sis a - ma - ra,
p
mi - hi non sis, a - ma - ra non
p
p
72
fac — me te - cum, fac me te - cum plan - ge - re, fac me
fac — me te cum, te - cum. fac me te - cum plan - ge - re, fac me
fac — me te - cum, fac me te - cum, fac me te - cum plan - ge - re, fac me
fac — me te - cum, fac me te - - cum, fac me te - cum plan - ge - re, fac me
sis, fac, fac, fac me te cum
f
f
f p
f

82
te - cum plan - ge - re.
te - cum plan - ge - re.
te - cum plan - ge - re.
te - cum plan - ge - re.
te - cum plan - ge - re.
89
SOLO
Fac, ut por - tem Chri - sti mor - tem,
SOLO
Fac, ut por - tem Chri - sti mor - tem,
p

97
pas - si - o - nis fac con - sor - tem,
SOLO
Fac, ut por - tem Chri - sti_ mor - tem,
pas - si - o - nis fac con - sor - tem,
SOLO
Fac, ut por - tem Chri - sti_ mor - tem,
106
pas - si - o - nis fac con - sor - tem,
pas - si - o - nis fac con - sor - tem, pas - si - o - nis fac con - sor - tem,
pas - si - o - nis fac con -
pas - si - o - nis fac con - sor - tem, pas - si - o - nis fac con -
f
Fac,
f
p
f p

116
et pla - gas, et pla - gas, et pla - gas, et pla - gas re - co - le - re.
et pla - gas, et pla - gas, et pla - gas, et pla - gas re - co - le - re.
sor - tem, et pla - gas, et pla - gas, et pla - gas, pla - gas re - co - le - re.
sor - tem, et pla - gas, et pla - gas, et pla-gas re - co - - le - re.
fac, et pla - gas re - co - le - re.
et pla-gas re - co - le - re.
(f p)
f
p
126
SOLO
Fac, ut por - tem Chri - sti mor - tem, pas - si - o - nis fac con - sor - tem,
p
pas - si -
p
p

135
p
et plagas, plagas recolere, et plagas plagas recole-
et plagas, plagas recolere, et plagas plagas recole-
et plagas recolere, et plagas recole-
et plagas recolere, plagas recole-
-onis fac consortem,
144
f
-re. Fac, fac, ut portem Christi mortem,
-re. Fac, fac, ut portem Christi mortem,
-re. Fac, fac, ut portem Christi mortem,
-re. Fac, fac, ut portem Christi mortem,
fac, fac, ut portem Christi mortem,
tr

150
pas - si - o - nis fac con - sor - tem et pla - gas re - co - le - re,
pas - si - o - nis fac con - sor - tem et pla - gas re - co - le - re,
pas - si - o - nis fac con - sor - tem et pla - gas re - co - le - re,
pas - si - o - nis fac con - sor - tem et pla - gas re - co - le - re,
fac, fac, et
p
f
p
158
pla - gas, pla - gas re - co - le - re.
pla - gas, pla - gas re - co - le - re.
pla - gas, pla - gas re - co - le - re.
pla - gas, pla - gas re - co - le - re.
pla - gas, pla - gas re - co - le - re.
f

164
Fac
me
pla
Fac
me
pla
p
171
gis
vul
ne
ra
ri,
gis
vul
ne
ra
ri,
Fac
me
pla
gis
vul
ne
ra
Fac
me
pla
gis
vul
ne
ra
Fac,
fac,
fac,

180
fac me pla - gis, pla - gis vul - ne -
fac me pla - gis, pla - gis vul - ne -
-ri, fac me pla - gis vul - ne -
-ri, fac me vul - ne -
cru - ce hac in - e - bri - a - ri
p
f
189
-ra-ri, cru - ce, cru - ce hac in - e - bri - a - ri, fac, fac,
-ra - ri, cru - ce, cru - ce hac in - e - bri - a - ri, fac, fac,
-ra - ri, cru - ce hac in - e - bri - a - ri, fac, fac,
-ra - ri, cru - ce in - e - bri - a - ri, fac, fac,
pla-gis me fac, pla-gis me fac,
p
f

197
ob a-mo - - rem fi-li-i,
ob a-mo-rem fi-li-i,
ob a-mo-rem fi-li-i,
ob a-mo - - rem fi-li-i,
ob a-mo - - rem
cru-ce in-e-bri-a-ri,
ob a-mo-rem
ob a-mo - - rem
206
cru-ce hac in-e-bri-a-ri, ob a-mo-rem fi-li-i,
cru-ce hac in-e-bri-a-ri, ob a-mo-rem fi-li-i,
cru-ce hac in-e-bri-a-ri, ob a-mo-rem fi-li-i,
cru-ce hac in-e-bri-a-ri, ob a-mo-rem fi-li-i,
fi-li-i,

215
cru - ce hac in - e - bri - a - ri, ob a - mo - rem fi - li - i.
cru - ce hac in - e - bri - a - ri, ob a - mo - rem fi - li - i.
cru - ce hac in - e - bri - a - ri, ob a - mo - rem fi - li - i.
cru - ce hac in - e - bri - a - ri, ob a - mo - rem fi - li - i.
cru - ce hac in - e - bri - a - ri, ob a - mo - rem fi - li - i.
223
Fac me pla - gis vul - ne - ra - ri, cru - ce hac in - e - bri - a - ri.
pla - gis me

232
Fac me pla-gis
Fac me pla-gis
Fac me pla-gis
Fac me pla-gis
fac, pla-gis me fac,
240
vul-ne-ra-ri, fac— me pla-gis vul-ne-ra-ri, ob a-mo-rem fi-li-
vul-ne-ra-ri, fac— me pla-gis vul-ne-ra-ri, ob a-mo-rem fi-li-
vul-ne-ra-ri, fac me pla-gis vul-ne-ra-ri, ob a-mo-rem fi-li-
vul-ne-ra-ri, fac— me vul-ne-ra-ri, ob— a-mo-rem fi-li-
fac, fac, fac,

249
-i, ob a - mo - rem fi - li - i.
-i, ob a - mo - rem fi - li - i.
-i, ob a - mo - rem fi - li - i.
-i, ob a - mo - rem fi - li - i.
ob— a - mo-rem, a - mo - rem fi - li - i.
256
XI Presto
SVT
4

8
11
BASSI SOLO
Flam mis
p
14
or - ci ne suc - cen - dar, flam - mis ne suc -
17
- cen - - dar, per te,
f
p
20
vir - go, fac, de - fen - dar, fac, de - fen - dar in

23
di - e, in di - e, in di - e ju -
p
26
- di - - ci - i, in di - e ju -
poco f
p
29
- di - ci - i, ju - di - ci -
crescendo
32
- i.
f
35

38
Flam - mis or - ci ne suc - cen - dar, ne suc -
p
41
- cen - dar, per te, vir - go, fac, de -
f
p
44
- fen - dar in di - e ju -
poco f
47
- di - ci - i, in di - e ju - di - ci - i.
p
sf
p
50
Per te, vir - go, fac, de - fen - -

53
-dar. Flam - mis or - ci,
56
fac, de - fen - dar in di - e, in
59
-di - e ju - di - ci - i, in
62
di - e ju - di - ci - i, ju -
65
-di - ci - i.
68

XII
Moderato
TENORE SOLO
Fac me cru - ce cus - to - di-ri, mor - te Chri - sti
prae - mu - ni - ri, con - ser - va - ri gra - ti - a, con - ser - va - ri gra - - - - - - - - - - ti - a.
Fac me cru - ce cus - to - di - ri, mor - - - - - - te
p
f

18
Chri - sti prae - mu-ni - ri, con - ser-va - ri gra - - - - - -
22
- - - - - - ti-a. Fac me cru-ce cus-to-di - ri, mor -
26
- te prae-mu-ni - ri, con-ser- va - ri, gra - - - - - - - - - -
30
- - - - - - ti-a, gra - ti -
34
- a.

XIIIa Largo assai

SOPRANO SOLO

Quan - do cor - pus

ALTO SOLO

Quan - do cor - pus mo - ri - e - tur, mo - ri - e - tur, mo - ri -

p

5

mo - ri - e - tur, quan - do cor - pus mo - ri - e - - - - - tur,

e - tur, mo - ri - e - tur, mo - ri - e - - - tur,

9 TUTTI

p fac, fac, *f* fac, ut a - ni - mae do - ne - tur, fac, ut

TUTTI

p fac, fac, *f* fac, ut a - ni - mae do - ne - tur, fac, ut

p fac, fac, *f* fac, ut a - ni - mae do - ne - tur, fac, ut

p fac, fac, *f* fac, ut a - ni - mae do - ne - tur, fac, ut

p *f*

12
a - ni-mae do - ne - tur Pa - ra - di - si,
a - ni-mae do - ne - tur Pa - ra - di - si,
a - ni-mae do - ne - tur Pa - ra - di - si,
a - ni-mae do - ne - tur Pa - ra - di - si,
14
Pa - ra - di - si glo - - - - - - - ri - a.
Pa - ra - di - si glo - ri - a, glo - - ri - a.
Pa - ra - di - si glo - - - - - - - ri - a.
Pa - ra - di - si glo - - - - - - - ri - a.
XIIIb
Alla breve
SOPRANO
ALTO
TENORE
BASSO
TUTTI
f
Pa - ra - di - si
Pa - ra - di - si glo - ri - a ut a - ni - mae do - ne - tur, A - men, A - - -
tr

26
Pa - ra -
glo - ri - a ut a - ni - mae do - ne - tur, A - men, A
men, A -
34
1 2 f
P Pa - ra - di - si
-di - si glo - ri - a ut a - ni - mae do - ne - tur, A - men, A
men, A
men.
42
glo - ri - a ut a - ni - mae do - ne - tur, A - men, A
men, A -
- men.
Pa - ra -

50
men. Pa - ra - di - si glo - ri -
Pa - ra - di - si glo - ri - a, A - -
di - si glo - ri - a ut a - ni - mae do - ne - tur, A - men, A - -
58
-men, A - - men, A - -
-a, A - - men, A - - men, A - -
-men, A - - men, A - - men, A - -
-men, A - - men, A - -
66
- men, A - - men, A - - men.
-men, A - - - men, A - - men.
- - men, A - - men, A - men.
- men, A - - - men.

74
SOPRANO SOLO
A
sim.
sim.
81
88
men.
A
Pa - ra
Pa - ra
94
TUTTI
Pa - ra - di - si, Pa - ra - di - si glo - ri - a,
men.
di - si glo - ri - a ut a - ni - mae do - ne - tur, A - men,
di - si glo - ri - a, A

101
A - men, A - - - - men.
Pa - ra - di - si
A
- - men, A - - - - - - - - - men,
108
Pa - ra - di - si glo - ri - a, A
glo - ri - a, A
men, A
A - - - men, A
115
- men, A
- men.
A
- men.

122
- - men,
A -
- - men, A - - - - - - men, A - - - - -
- - men, A - - - - - - - - - - - - men.
Pa - ra - di - si glo - ri - a ut a - ni - mae do - ne - tur,
129
- - - - - - - - - - - men, A - - - - -
- - - - - - - - - - - men, A - -
Pa - ra - di - si glo - ri -
A - - - - - - - - - - - - - - men,
136
- - - - - - - - - - - - - - - - - -
- men. Pa - ra - di - si glo - ri - a, A - men.
- a, A - - - - - - - - - - - - -
A - - - - - - - - - men, A -

143
-men. Pa - ra - di - - si glo - ri - a,
Pa - ra - di - - si glo - ri - a, A - - - - - - -
-men. Pa - ra - di - si glo - ri - a, A - - - - - - -
-men, A - - - - - - - - - -
150
SOLO
A - - - men. A - - - - - - -
- - - - - - men.
- - - men, A - - men.
- - - men, A - men.
p
sim.
157
164
tr

171
TUTTI
SOLO
-men. A - - - - - - - - - - - men, A - -
SOLO
A - men, A - - men, A - men, A - -
A - - men, A - - - - - - men, A - men.
A - - - - - - - - - - - - men, A - men.
178
TUTTI
SOLO
- - - - men. A - - men. A - -
TUTTI
SOLO
- - - - men. A - - men. A - -
SOLO
TUTTI
A - - - - - men, A - - men.
SOLO
TUTTI
A - - - - - men, A - - men.
184
TUTTI
- - men, A - men, A - men.
TUTTI
- - men, A - men, A - men.
SOLO
TUTTI
A - - - men, A - men, A - men.
SOLO
TUTTI
A - - - men, A - men, A - men.